That's Exerc...

Written by Cassie Bell

Illustrated by Antony Bunyan

I like
to exercise.

2

I ride
my bicycle
to school.
That's exercise!

3

I run
to the finish line.
That's exercise!

4

I swim
in the swimming pool.
That's exercise!

5

I walk
my puppy to the park.
That's exercise!

6

I skip
to my friend's house.
That's exercise!

I have had
a lot of exercise today.
And now I am very tired!

8